Life's Not Always Fair

A Child's Guide to Managing Emotions

Sharon Scott, L.P.C., L.M.F.T.
with Nicholas, the Cocker Spaniel

Illustrated by
George Phillips

HRD Press, Amherst, Massachusetts

Published by Human Resource Development Press, Inc.
22 Amherst Road
Amherst, Massachusetts 01002
(413) 253-3488
1-800-822-2801 (U.S. and Canada)
(413) 253-3490 (fax)
http://www.hrdpress.com

ISBN 0-87425-399-3

Dedicated with love to my faithful
Nicholas
for giving friendship, teachings, and joy to so many

Everything I Need to Know about Life
I Learned from My Cocker Spaniel
Nicholas

♡ Good dogs finish first ♡ **Be loyal** ♡ Have dog-day afternoons lying in the sun ♡ **Make time to play with your toys** ♡ Bark loudly only when you need to protect others ♡ **Don't gossip** ♡ Be kind to others ♡ **When it's a dog-eat-dog day, go for a walk** ♡ Groom yourself daily ♡ **A friendly wag (smile) will get you somewhere** ♡ Know when to be a hushpuppy ♡ **Appreciate cats—and all those who are different from you** ♡ Don't bark up the wrong tree ♡ **Accept your siblings even when they irritate you** ♡ When you're dog-tired, curl up and have sweet dreams ♡ **Eat a fruit snack every day** ♡ Be man's and woman's best friend ♡ **Don't play too "ruff"** ♡ Always give enthusiastic greetings ♡ **Don't go out without ID** ♡ It's good to have more than one friend ♡ **You're never too old to learn new tricks** ♡ Volunteer work is good ♡ **Every day, kiss those you love most** ♡

Other Books by Sharon Scott

Peer Pressure Reversal: An Adult Guide to Developing a
Responsible Child, Second Edition

How to Say No and Keep Your Friends, Second Edition

Positive Peer Groups

When to Say Yes! And Make More Friends

Other Books by Sharon Scott and Nicholas, the Cocker Spaniel

Too Smart for Trouble

Not Better . . . Not Worse . . . Just Different

Too Cool for Drugs (co-authored by Dr. Wayne Hindmarsh)

Table of Contents

About the Authors

Sharon Scott is a licensed professional counselor and marriage and family therapist whose internationally recognized work has been making a difference in people's lives for over 25 years. From the home base of her private practice near Dallas, Texas, she has traveled extensively, providing keynote speeches and workshops for schools, hospitals, social service agencies, religious organizations, and law enforcement agencies. She has brought her Peer Pressure Reversal program—one of the most highly respected refusal programs in the nation—to over one million people across the United States and in Australia, Canada, Malaysia, and Micronesia. Her seven years of service as Director of the Dallas Police Department's First Offender Program helped shape that program into a national model for delinquency prevention.

She is also the author of seven other widely acclaimed books. She has been quoted on television programs and in numerous publications, including *USA Today, 20/20, Good Housekeeping, Teen Magazine, Scholastic Choices, Newsweek,* and *The Washington Post,* and has appeared on *CNN* and *Good Morning Australia.*

Nicholas, Sharon's beloved Cocker Spaniel, is her "co-author." He loves children and enjoys accompanying Sharon when she makes presentations at elementary schools. Upon entering a classroom, Nicholas is able to sense which child has the greatest need and will seek out that child to greet first! His professional work has earned him a listing in the 1995 *Who's Who of Dogs*. Nicholas has also visited nursing homes as a pet therapy dog and has worked as a volunteer for the humane society.

Sharon and Nicholas were honored by the Texas Counseling Association with the 1995 "Professional Writing Award" for their three previous books.

Preface

With the increase of violence in our society, the "in your face" language and disrepectful attitudes of people of all ages, the inability of young and old to manage their emotions, and the cynicism that has resulted from these problems, it has become **imperative** for us to teach young children **how** to deal with stressful situations. We must help them learn how to cope in positive, life-affirming ways with difficult emotions—such as anger, sadness, fear, or confusion—as well as how to handle happy emotions without appearing to be "showing off."

To address this important issue, Nicholas (my real-life Cocker Spaniel) and I have once again joined forces, basing *Life's Not Always Fair* on actual events in the lives of Nicholas and his animal friends. Complete with problem-solving exercises and easy-to-follow suggestions, this volume helps children develop strategies for coping with stressful situations and maintaining emotional well-being. Emotional intelligence is crucial to help children thrive and succeed. Fortunately, it can be learned and improved!

Maybe we adults, too, will learn more about managing our emotions as we read along with our children! Let's hope so.

Special thanks to the following people who helped prepare this book:

- George Phillips for the fabulous illustrations
- HRD Press staff for great suggestions
- Our young "editors": Stephen Hurley, grade 5; Lauren Burkert, grade 1; Brian Zelman, grade 3; Kevin Claborn, grade 4; Casey Ernsberger, grade 2; Jeffrey Luse, grade 3; Brent Green, grade K; Kathryn Luse, grade 6; and Jordan Murphy, grade 5

- Dr. Jerry Rubin and Dr. Catherine Lustgarten for making time for the medical photos
- Judy Holder, elementary school counselor, and Elizabeth Luse, elementary school teacher, for their valuable comments
- My father, Harry V. Scott, Jr., and my husband, John Przywara, for taking the photographs in which I appear

Dallas, Texas
December 1995   Sharon Scott

An Important Note to Parents and Teachers

This book will be most effective for your child or student if you follow these suggestions:

1. First, read the book by yourself. You will be attempting to teach your child or student valuable skills needed to manage difficult emotions; therefore, it might be interesting to the child if you begin by relating a situation in which you had difficulty dealing with anger, sadness, or similar emotions. Tell the child that this book has some good ideas about how to handle those tough times that we all have.
2. Then read the book to, or with, the child. The comprehension of young children varies greatly, so you may need to elaborate on certain points to help the child understand them. I have "field-tested" the book on children and found it best for those in grades 1 through 5.
3. Slowly work through the book together, reading no more than one chapter at a time. Engage in some light discussion about what was read. You could have the child tell what he or she learned to another adult or to a friend, doll, or dog. Or you could have the child make a drawing for you about it.
4. Avoid lecturing while reading (e.g., "You really lose your temper a lot, so listen to this." Or, "Remember when you were scared to sing when you were in the play? You're too old to feel that way.") Do not use this book to discipline the child for not managing his or her feelings. It should always be used on a positive note.
5. Chapters 7 and 8 give the child practice in thinking about personal feelings and exercising the techniques learned in this book.
6. Read with enthusiasm and emotion in your voice. I and five animal characters "talk" in this book. It would really be fun if you could use a slightly different voice for each one!

An Important Note to Parents and Teachers (Continued)

7. Teaching transparencies and a Nicholas puppet are available to assist educators and other professional helpers in teaching this material. See page 110 for details on ordering.

Chapter 1
Tales or Tails?

Typing the tales.

Hi! My name is Nicholas. I am a ten-year-old Cocker Spaniel. A Cocker Spaniel is a kind of dog. I live near Dallas, Texas, with my mother, father, two brothers, and two sisters. I have long, blonde hair and brown eyes. My birthday is April 20. My favorite things to do are play with my toys and go for a walk in the park. I also like to eat—especially snacks like apples, oranges, or pears. I even like to eat broccoli!

What do you look like?

When is your birthday?

What do you like to do for fun?

What are your favorite snacks?

Oh, yes, and I love to write books. I really do! In fact, this is the fourth book that I've written.

One book I wrote was about making good decisions. Another book I wrote was about being kind to others. And the third book I wrote was about not using drugs. Those are all important things to know.

This book is about something different. It is about our **feelings**.

What are feelings?

Feelings are your moods or your emotions. Feelings are how you feel inside.

There are different kinds of feelings. Some names for the way you feel are **happy**, **sad**, **mad**, **scared**, and **confused**.

Some feelings feel great! When you feel happy or excited or silly or proud, you feel wonderful inside. These are **up** feelings.

You will smile, laugh, and be relaxed. You won't have a care in the world!

There are many, many things that make you feel happy. You are happy when you go to a birthday party. You are excited when you're having fun playing with your friends. You feel good when you're reading a book with your parent or grandparent.

Happy feelings are great. This is a feeling that you will learn to have more and more. You will want to be happy a lot!

Other feelings make you feel bad inside. When you feel scared, you may feel shaky inside. When you feel sad, you may feel like crying. Feeling mad is also a yucky, terrible feeling. And feeling confused is an uncomfortable feeling because you don't know what to do. These are **down** feelings.

You probably have some of these feelings almost every day. You might feel scared when you have to talk in front of the class. Or you might be sad because your best friend has moved away. You might be mad if someone calls you a mean name. You might feel confused when you don't understand how to do your homework.

Everyone has all kinds of different feelings every day.

'Down' feelings

sad

confused

mad

scared

This book is about how to have happy feelings a lot of the time.

I know you don't want to feel bad for long. So you'll learn how to turn your down feelings into up feelings. Then you'll feel good again. Yea!

All feelings are OK to have. But it's important to handle them correctly. You want to handle them so that you don't hurt yourself or anyone else. This book will help you learn how to **change** feelings of being sad, mad, scared, or confused into better feelings.

I'm going to tell you some tales about . . .

What is all the noise?

It's just my brothers and sisters coming in from playing outside.

"What are you doing, Nicholas?" asked Cedric, my brother who is an orange cat. "Still working on your book?"

"Yes," I said. "I'm going to tell the boys and girls some tales about feelings."

"I have a tail! It curls over my back," said Mandy, my sister who is a spotted dog.

"I have a tail, too! Mine is fluffy," said Katy. Katy is my baby sister and is a calico cat.

My little brother, Alexander, who is a Cocker Spaniel puppy, said, "I have a tail, too. It's short and it wags a lot!"

"I'm not talking about tails. I'm talking about **tales**!" I said.

"Huh?" said Cedric, Mandy, Katy, and Alexander.

I took a deep breath and tried again. "I'm going to tell some **tales**, not tails."

"What do you mean?" asked Mandy.

"Explain yourself," said Katy.

Cedric added, "You're not making sense, Nicholas."

Alexander said, "Huh?"

I told them that the tails on their bodies are spelled t-a-i-l-s. I was not going to talk about those.

I explained, "I'm going to tell some tales spelled t-a-l-e-s. Tales are stories. These stories will be about our feelings."

"Oh," they said. Then Katy added, "My tail is fluffy and beautiful."

"Oh, my," I said. "How can I explain this? I think it's going to be a **very** long day!"

Chapter 2
Katy's Tale

Katy feels confused.

Katy started telling us about her big, fluffy tail, which stands up tall when she walks.

She said, "Nicholas, look at my tail. It's soft, and I can curl it around me when I get cold."

"I know, Katy," I said. "But listen very carefully. This book is about tales, not tails! I know those words sound alike, but they are spelled differently. So they mean different things."

"Oh," said Katy. "Tell me again what your book is about."

"Gladly," I said. "This book is about tales, or stories, and the tales are about our feelings. We're going to talk about how to change down feelings into better feelings. That way we can be happy more often."

Katy said, "I had a bad feeling when Mommy brought Alexander home to live with us."

"How did you feel, Katy?" I asked.

"I felt confused," she said.

"Why did you feel confused, Katy?" I asked.

"Well, I was the baby in the family. You're ten, Nicholas. Mandy is thirteen. Cedric is seven years old. And I am only three. So I was the youngest and everybody gave me lots of attention. I liked being the baby.

"Alexander was a cute baby puppy when Mommy brought him home. I was afraid that Mommy would love Alexander more than she loved me. She spent a lot of time with him. And so did Daddy. It seemed like they were playing with him all the time. And they took pictures of him. They gave him new toys. I worried a lot about it. I didn't know what to do."

I asked Katy if it felt good to be confused, and she said no.

So I asked, "Katy, did you try to do anything to get rid of those mixed-up, confused feelings?"

"Not at first, Nicholas. I just worried about what to do. I'd lay awake at night trying to figure it out."

"Did worrying help, Katy?" I said.

"No, not really," she said. "So I finally decided to do something about it. I asked Mommy if I could talk to her about my confused feelings."

"Great idea, Katy. That was smart thinking! If we have confused feelings about another person, it is a good idea to talk to that person about them. Talking about your feelings can help solve the problem. What happened when you talked to Mom?"

Katy said, "I told Mommy that I was confused. I said I thought she loved Alexander more than she loved me. Mommy picked me up and hugged me. She said that she loved all of us. She said that she didn't love any one of us more than the other. She also said that I was special to her. Mommy said she loved me because of how gentle I am. She said she likes it when she's brushing her hair and I want her to brush my hair too. She said she thinks it's funny when I hide in baskets or cabinets around the house."

"Did your talk make you feel better?" I asked.

"It did. In fact, Mommy explained why she and Daddy had to spend lots of time with Alexander. She said that because he was a baby, he wouldn't learn how to behave if they didn't teach him lots of stuff."

Katy added, "Mommy said they had to teach him to take turns, to play nicely, and not to tear up things. That's when I understood that my parents needed to teach him to be a good dog. When he learns these things, our family is happier. Then I understood that Mommy and Daddy love us all so much. And there may be times when Mommy and Daddy need to spend some extra time with each of us."

"Golly, Katy," I said, "it sounds like your confused feelings went away. When you decided to ask Mommy if you could talk to her about your feelings, you took the first step toward changing them.

"So one way to get rid of confused feelings is to talk about the feelings. Explain how you feel and why. Most people will listen and will try to help you."

Here are three suggestions that can help us change confused feelings into better feelings:

 Ask questions.

 Talk about your feelings. If you feel confused about a person, talk to that person about it.

 Make a chart to solve the problem.

1. Ask Questions

If you feel confused because you are going to be in a new situation, it is important to **Ask Questions**. Try to learn more about the situation by asking questions. That way you'll know what to expect.

For example, if you're worried about what your first visit to the doctor will be like, then **Ask Questions**. Ask your parents how long you will be there and what the doctor will do. Ask your friends if any of them have been to the doctor. You'll find out how easy it is.

Or, if you're confused about what your new school will be like, then **Ask Questions**. Ask your parents what it will be like. Ask if they will drive you by the new school so you can see it before your first day there. Maybe you can even visit the school one day and meet some of the children that go to the school.

2. Talk about Your Feelings

If you're feeling confused about another person, try **Talking to That Person**. Ask the person if you can talk to him or her—just like when Katy asked to talk to her mom.

Tell the person why you are confused. Also tell the person that you want to solve the problem. Maybe he or she will want to talk to you, too. Talking things out can often help make the confused feelings go away.

3. Make a Chart

Another way that you can try to make confused feelings go away is to **Make a Chart** to solve the problem. If you are mixed-up about what to do, you can list your choices at the top of the chart. Then you write down all the good things and all the bad things about each choice. This helps you use your brain to look at the situation carefully.

For example, Jim's parents are going to let him sign up for a fun activity. He is not sure whether to join a baseball team or to take guitar lessons. He wants to do both, but he has permission to be involved in only one activity. How does he decide which one is best for him? By **Making a Chart** to help him solve the problem. Look at the chart Jim made.

Baseball
Good stuff:
1. Make new friends.
2. Get exercise.

Not so good stuff:
1. Practice three times a week.
2. Can't miss games or practices.
3. Games are on the weekend so I can't see my friends.
4. Practice is far from my house.

Guitar lessons
Good stuff:
1. Lessons are only once a week.
2. I will have my very own teacher so I will get lots of help.
3. I can already play the guitar a little.
4. I like music!
5. I can change time of lessons.
6. Class is only three blocks away.

Not so good stuff:
1. Guitar is expensive to buy.

Jim's Problem-Solving Chart

	Choice 1 — Baseball	Choice 2 — Guitar
Good Reasons	1. Make new friends. 2. Get exercise.	1. Lesson is only once a week. 2. I will have my very own teacher, so I will get lots of help. 3. Already can play the guitar a little. 4. I like music! 5. Can change time of lesson. 6. Class is only 3 blocks away.
Bad Reasons	1. Meets three times a week. 2. Can't miss games or practice. 3. Games are on the weekends, so I can't see my friends. 4. Practice is far from my house.	1. Guitar is expensive to buy.

After looking at the many good reasons to take guitar lessons, Jim may decide to do just that. Jim also sees there are four problems with joining a baseball team. There is only one problem with taking guitar lessons—money. Jim's parents have told him they could find a used guitar, which costs less money than a new one. After talking to his parents, he decides that taking guitar lessons is a better choice.

So Jim signs up for lessons. He is no longer confused about what he wants to do! **Making a Chart** made the decision easier!

Remember, there are three ideas to try acting on when you want confused feelings to go away:

• Ask questions.

• Talk about your feelings. If you feel confused about a person, talk to that person about it.

• Make a chart to solve the problem.

Isn't it a good feeling when you know how to make confused feelings go away? **You** are in control of your own feelings. If you don't like feeling confused, you—and only you—can change the feeling!

That's how life works.

Chapter 3
Cedric's Tale

Cedric is sad.

Cedric said, "If Katy has finished telling you about her tail, I want to tell you about mine. My tail is orange, like the rest of my body. It's long and stands up high. Many times it looks like a question mark as I hold it curved on top, like this:

"Cedric," I said, "Didn't you hear what I told Katy? This book is about tales, spelled t-a-l-e-s. Tales are stories. Do you have an interesting story about a feeling that you've had?"

"As a matter of fact, I do," he said. Cedric got tears in his eyes and slowly, softly started to tell this true story . . .

"When I was seven weeks old," Cedric said, 'I was left at the animal pound. I was put in a small cage with food and water. The people that worked at the pound were very nice to me, but I was so lonely. I wanted a family to take me home to live with them.

"One week went by and no one took me home. Then two weeks went by. I was really sad. Three weeks passed, then four weeks and five weeks went by. I was feeling hopeless. Six weeks came and went, but on the seventh week . . . "

"A nice-looking man walked into the front office. I could hear him tell the people that worked at the pound that he wanted to get a kitten as a surprise birthday present for his wife. I crossed my paws for luck and wished that he would pick me.

"There were lots of nice kittens available, and he looked at each of us. When he came to my cage, I said 'Meow.' Then I slipped my paw out of the cage and touched his arm.

"He began talking to me and asked if I wanted to go home with him. Boy, did I ever! And so I went home with him."

"Dad handed the box—with me inside—to Mom. She was so surprised and happy to have me. Mom introduced me to the rest of the family. She introduced me to you, Nicholas, and to the other two dogs, Mandy and Shawn.

"Nicholas, you and Mandy had never seen a cat before. You both barked at me at first and didn't seem to know what I was. It took you two a while before you liked me. But Shawn had a cat friend when he was a young dog and knew what I was. So he welcomed me right away. Shawn was so kind to me. As you know, he became my very, very best friend."

Cedric and Shawn were best buddies.

Cedric went on, "Shawn and I played together. He let me rub my head on his, and I often slept curled up next to him. We were best buddies.

"Shawn got to be an old dog and became sick. His heart would not work right. We went to the veterinarian—or "vet," for short—a lot. A vet is a doctor who cares for animals.

"One day when he was very old, Shawn died. He just quit breathing. I wanted to play with him some more, but there would be no more times to do that. I missed him so much."

"Cedric, how did you feel when Shawn died?" I asked.

"Sad. Very, very sad," Cedric answered.

I asked Cedric how sad feelings feel inside.

He said, "I felt like crying all the time. I felt all alone even though people were around me. I felt empty inside. Feeling sad is a lonely feeling."

"What did you do to try to make the sad feelings go away?" I asked.

Cedric said, "At first I wouldn't even let anyone try to help me. Whenever Mom tried to pick me up to hug me, I would pull away from her. I didn't want to eat my food. I felt so sad that I didn't know what to do."

I said, "There will be a lot of times when we feel sad, so it's important that we learn how to make sad feelings become less sad. Cedric, what did you finally do that helped you change your sad feelings?"

He said, "Well, I started carrying a stuffed animal around the house. I didn't have Shawn to curl up next to, so I tried curling up next to the stuffed animal—and it helped me feel better. I also ate even though I didn't feel like it. And I began to talk to Mom about how much I missed Shawn. We both cried because we missed him, but it was a good cry because it let us get our feelings out. Mom would give me a big hug. We would talk about all the good times we had with Shawn. That helped us remember the fun times and made us feel better."

I told Cedric that he was very smart to try to change his sad feelings into better ones. He—and only he—can take charge of his feelings and try to make himself feel less sad.

There are many ways that we can comfort ourselves. Here are three very good ways:

1. Ask for a hug from someone or something that you love. It could be your parent, grandparent, pet, or even a stuffed animal. Hugs can help make us feel better when we are sad.

2. Keep a journal of your feelings. A journal is your very own personal notebook in which you write or draw your thoughts. Each day write or draw how you feel that day and why you feel that way.

This can help you see that you have more happy days than sad days. So when you have a sad day, you know that there will be happy days to come! A journal might look like this:

3. Talk to an adult whom you trust. It could be your mom or dad, grandparent, aunt or uncle, or your teacher. People that care about you will listen. When someone understands your feelings and is willing to help you, it can make you feel better.

There might be a counselor at your school. Their job is to help people who have a problem and to listen when someone needs to talk. So when you are very sad, another thing to do is ask your teacher if you can talk to the counselor.

An adult whom you trust will always do what is best for you. A trusted adult is never hurtful toward you and would never ask you to keep a bad secret.

School Counselor

Counselors listen with their hearts

Chapter 4
Mandy's Tale

Mandy gets rid of her mad feelings.

My sister Mandy had been listening to Cedric's tale about missing Shawn. She said, "I miss Shawn, too. He was a good brother and so kind." Mandy wiped a tear from her eye, then said, "Nicholas, I'm sure you've noticed my tail. It is the most unusual because it curls up over my back!"

"Oh, no," I said." Here we go again! Mandy, have you been napping? I've explained many times that this book is about tales and that the tales are about feelings. It's not about the tails on our bodies!"

"I'm sorry. I forgot. That's what happens when you get older. You forget more. I'm 13 in dog years, but that is 75 in people years!"

"No problem, Mandy. Do you have a tale about your feelings?"

"I get mad easily. Then I lose my temper. I don't like feeling mad! When I'm mad, my heart beats fast and I get out of breath. I feel hot and sometimes my head hurts. My stomach feels like it has knots in it. It feels terrible to be mad."

"What makes you mad?" I asked.

"Lots of things," Mandy answered. "Sometimes I get a little mad at Alexander when he tries to play while I'm trying to sleep. He jumps on my head and nips at my feet. He can be such a pest."

"I know Alexander bothers you," I said. "He's a puppy, and he's still learning when to play and how to play."

"Well, I'll be glad when he grows up," Mandy said.

"It won't be long," I told her.

Mandy kept talking. "And sometimes I get mad at Dad when he's too busy to take me for a walk before he goes to work. He lets me go in the backyard for a while. But I like to go for a walk in the front yard. It's more fun."

"You get frustrated, Mandy, when you don't get to do something that you look forward to."

"That's right. I know some days that Dad has to go to work early. He has a lot of important meetings. And he works hard to pay the bills so we can live in a nice house and have some toys.

"But what really makes me mad is when children tease me. Sometimes they climb up on our wooden fence in the backyard and look over at me. Then they make faces. Sometimes they make barking noises to upset me. And sometimes they have even pushed sticks through the holes in the fence to try to hit me.

"I don't know why they do this. I haven't done anything to them. I'm a nice dog and I've never hurt anyone. I'm in my own yard and they shouldn't be treating me this way!"

"You must be furious," I told Mandy. "What do you do when this happens?"

"I bark at them. But they don't go away. Mom has to come outside and ask them to leave me alone. She tells them to stop it. Then she asks them nicely to quit teasing me."

"Does that help?" I asked Mandy.

She said, "Yes, usually it helps."

"Children that are bullies are not acting nice," I said. "Usually they are upset about something in their lives and take it out on others. That is not the way to deal with their upset feeling!"

So, what have we learned from Mandy's tale?

We learned that barking back at someone—or yelling back as people do—does not help. In fact, it may make others angrier and then they may act meaner. When people yell at each other, fights can start. And that is no way to solve problems. No one can listen to someone else when a fight has started.

We also learned that if Mandy hadn't lost her temper so quickly, she might have solved the problem by standing up for herself. When someone is bothering you for no reason, tell them firmly, "Stop it! I don't like that. Quit acting mean!" Then walk away quickly. Don't cry. Don't yell. Don't hit. Don't look hurt. Usually the reason that the other person talks mean is because he or she is trying to show off to the other kids. The other person wants you to get upset, so don't let that happen. Stay in control of yourself.

Try this at least 5 times whenever a person talks mean to you for no reason. If it hasn't stopped after 5 times, it would be a good idea to ask for help from an adult whom you trust. Like Mandy did when she asked Mom for help.

Never keep angry feelings bottled up inside you. You'll feel like you'll explode. And you might take your anger out on the wrong person.

And **never** let your anger control you. Yelling, stomping your feet, kicking, throwing things, saying bad words, or hitting people or animals **never** solves the problem. Losing control of yourself will make the situation worse. And it will make you look weak.

So what do you do to change mad feelings?

Talk . . . talk . . . talk . . . and talk some more!

Whom do you talk to?

First, if the person toward whom you have the mad feelings is a friend, then try talking it out. Ask him or her if there is a time when the two of you can talk about the situation. Don't have other friends present—just the two of you need to work this out. Tell the person that you really want things to be better between the two of you. Then explain that if you both talk long enough, then maybe you both can work things out.

If the person agrees to talk with you, decide exactly when and where to meet. Make it the same day, if possible.

When you meet, tell the person that you both can take turns telling each other why you are mad. You should not interrupt each other. Then both of you can suggest ways to solve the problem. Decide which solution is best, and then follow through. Thank the other person for taking the time to talk.

Here is an easy way to remember what to do:

Step 1: Ask to talk, and set time and place.
Step 2: Take turns telling **why** you're mad.
Step 3: Listen and don't interrupt.
Step 4: Both of you suggest ways to solve the problem.
Step 5: Decide on the best solution—and do it!

Mandy said, "That's exactly what Mom did when she talked to the children who were teasing me! Mom told the children that I was mad and that teasing me was unkind. The children took their turn and said they were trying to play with me. Mom asked them if I looked like I was happy. They noticed I was jumping at the fence and barking. They agreed that I didn't think they were playing. The solution they both came up with was not to tease me through the fence. The children were told to come to the front door and ask permission whenever they wanted to play with me. Mom's so smart."

"Yes," I said. "In fact, let's call her in here and see if she has any more ideas on how to change mad feelings into better ones? Mom? Oh, Mom?"

"Yes, Nicholas. What's up?" she said.

"Can you help us talk about some ways to calm down angry feelings?" I asked. "Since you're a counselor who helps people with problems, I thought you would know some ways."

"Of course," Mom said. "First, when you're mad at a person, try talking to that person about your feelings. Listen to each other, and try to come up with solutions to the problem. Maybe you two misunderstood each other. Or maybe another person spread a lie about one of you. Or maybe you should just ignore each other and give yourselves time to cool off."

I said, "We've already talked about how important talking is. What other ideas do you have?"

"Lots," she said. And then she began telling us these other ways to calm down angry feelings:

☺ When you are angry, count to 10 before you speak. And take some big, deep breaths. That helps you think before you say something you don't really mean. You might even need to leave the room to give yourself time to calm down. Don't be mean to others when you're upset about something. Being a bully is acting weak.

☺ Draw a picture of how you feel. Then write on the picture: "Let's solve this problem and be friends." Give it to the person toward whom you have the mad feelings.

☺ If you have a pet, sit with your dog or cat or bird and tell it your problem. Pets listen and care about you.

☺ Find something that calms you down. Hug your dolls, or color, or hold your teddy bear. Or listen to your favorite kind of music.

☺ Read a book of jokes or a funny story.

☺ Splash your face with cool water.

☺ Go outside, with permission, and get some fresh air.

☺ Do something that tires you out. For example, ride your bike, sing, roller-blade, exercise, jump rope, or skate. Get rid of the angry energy.

☺ If you've done something unkind to cause the argument, apologize to the other person. If you can't face the person, then say that you're sorry in a letter.

☺ Tell yourself that you are too nice a person to stay mad for long.

"Wow!" I said. "Thanks, Mom, for those great ideas. There are lots of ways to cool down angry feelings. It doesn't always solve the problem, but it surely helps you feel better inside. Staying mad is a terrible way to feel. Now we have some things to try the next time we get mad. Which ones do you think will work best for you?"

Chapter 5
Nicholas' Tale

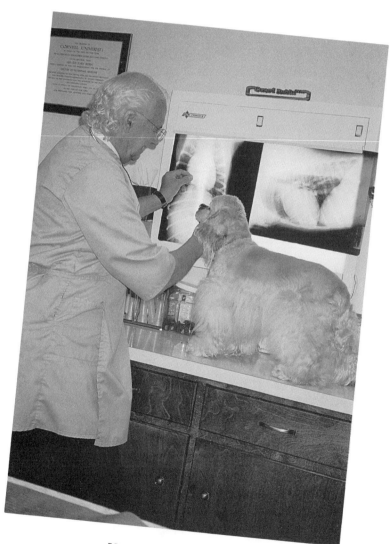

I'm scared.

"We've heard Katy's, Cedric's, and Mandy's tales, so now I want to tell you my tale. And don't **anyone** say anything about how mine wags all the time! Remember, we're talking about tales that are stories!"

"We remember!" said Cedric, Katy, Mandy, and Alexander.

Alexander, the puppy, asked, "Nicholas, is your tale about a feeling?"

"Yes, it is. A scared feeling."

"Who's feeling scared?" asked Mandy.

"I am. Very, very scared."

"What's wrong, Nicholas?" Cedric asked in a concerned voice.

And, so, I began to tell my true tale . . .

"I wasn't feeling well and one side of my nose was swollen. I was sneezing a lot and sometimes sneezing blood, so Mom took me to the vet."

"That can be scary," Katy said.

"Yes, because the vets did lots of tests on me. They took a little blood from my leg. They took x-rays, which are pictures of the inside of your body. The vets listened to my heart and felt the glands in my throat."

Katy said, "Did the tests hurt, Nicholas?"

"Some did, just a little bit. And others didn't hurt at all. For example, I didn't feel anything when the x-rays were taken. The doctors knew something was wrong with my nose, but couldn't tell for sure without doing an operation on it.

"The vets told me that I would be given some medicine to make me sleep for about one hour. That way I wouldn't feel them cutting on my nose. And they were right—I didn't feel anything during the operation.

"When I woke up, I was very sleepy and sore. What they found growing in my nose was not good—it was cancer. Cancer is a very serious disease.

"The vets explained to Mom and me what we could do to make me better. I was so scared. We went home, and later, Mom found me crying in my bed.

"Mom came into my room and sat next to my bed.

"'Nicholas, let's talk. I'm so sorry that you're sick. We need to decide what to do now. The doctor said he could give you some medicine, called chemotherapy, and use a special machine to give your nose radiation treatments. The doctor said this might make the cancer go away. But the doctor said this medicine could also make you sick to your stomach and cause the hair on your nose to fall out. What do you think you want to do?'

"I told Mom that I wanted to try to get rid of the cancer. So we started the many months of going to the doctor for these treatments. And I got sick to my stomach and, sure enough, the hair on my nose fell out. A few people stared at my nose which was rude. But most people have been nice and not teased me about it. And Mom has always been there with me to hold my paw."

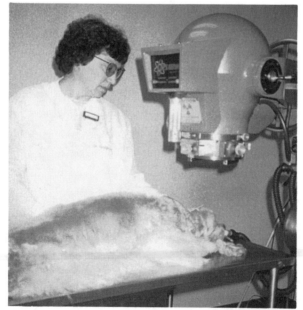

I'm getting ready for radiation treatment.

"This is hard to talk about," I sniffled.

Katy said, "I'll rub up against you, Nicholas. Maybe that will make you less sad."

Mandy said, "Nicholas, here's some water. Take a sip."

Alexander snuggled next to me, and Cedric patted my shoulder. Then Mom walked into the room.

"Nicholas, why are you all looking so sad?" she asked.

I replied, "I'm telling my brothers and sisters about my cancer."

Mom said, "Nicholas, you have been very brave during your treatments. I'm so proud of you. And I love you so much." She gave me a big hug and held me in her lap. Then she asked, "Is there something else on your mind?"

"Yes," I said. "Why did this have to happen to me? I've always been a good dog. And I've tried to help people and other animals. Sometimes I visit schools with you, Mom, to talk to the children. And I've visited lots of nursing homes and cheered up the older people living there. And I've done volunteer work trying to get families that want a pet to adopt a homeless animal from the animal shelter. How come this bad disease had to happen to me?"

Mom kept holding me as she said, "Nicholas, you **have** always been a good boy. And you have helped so many people. And so many children love your books. They write you nice letters that we have put in your scrapbook. So many people have sent you get-well cards. And one friend even named her new puppy after you. You **are** good!

"But sometimes bad things happen to good dogs—and good people, too. You didn't do anything to cause this bad disease to happen to you. It just happened. Life's not always fair."

I said to Mom, "I don't really understand."

Mom said, "I don't either, Nicholas. Good and bad things happen to all of us—not only to people, but to little animals too. When good things happen, appreciate them and feel great. When bad things happen, just do your best to get through them. Sometimes others say mean things about us for no reason. Sometimes accidents happen. Sometimes our best friends quit liking us and we don't even know why. And sometimes we get sick. But better days will come.

"When these things happen, share your feelings with your family and close friends. They will comfort you like your brothers and sisters are doing for you now. And it's OK to cry, too. That is the way our body says, 'I'm scared' or 'I'm sad.'

"Also, when you're scared, get hugged. If necessary, **ask** for hugs from those you love. Hug your parent. Hug your grandparent. Hug your pet. Even hug your stuffed animals! It really does help you when you know that someone else cares."

Then Mom hugged me tighter. And I did feel better.

Alexander is happy.

"Once upon a tale . . ." began Alexander, the puppy.

I said, "What?"

Alexander answered, "Nicholas, I'm starting to tell my tale about a feeling."

I told him that he was being silly and acting like a baby.

Alexander said, "Well, I **am** a baby. And I'm trying not to be silly by not telling you about my tail that wags all the time, even when I'm asleep."

"Oh, yeah. I forgot how young you are," I said. "Go ahead with your tale, Alexander. You can begin it anyway you want."

"OK. Once upon a tale . . ." Alexander began.

Alexander tells his tale.

". . . there was a little blonde puppy. He was so cute and sweet!"

"Are you talking about yourself?" I asked.

Alexander said, "Yes, I am! As you know, Mommy brought me home to live with all of you when I was just seven weeks old. I was scared and cried the whole time that mom was driving me home. Then I cried for two more days because I was young and didn't understand what was going on. But you all were so nice to me.

"Cedric, you taught me how to play wrestle on the floor. What fun! And, Mandy, you were curious about me. Katy, you taught me not to be so rough, and to play easy. I'm still working on that! And, Nicholas, you let me curl up next to you to sleep."

I can't sleep because of Alexander wiggling!

"Thank you," I told Alexander. "You were our new baby brother, and we wanted to make you feel welcome."

"You did," said Alexander. "But I also know that I made quite a few mistakes. When I started losing my baby teeth, my gums hurt. I tried to chew on the furniture—and even on your long ears, Nicholas! And when I was through in the backyard and wanted to go back inside the house, I howled at the top of my voice! I didn't know that I was supposed to tap on the door with my paw."

"That was funny," I said. "We thought something got a hold of you. You were **so** loud!

"And don't forget how you thought everything was a toy—and was yours! You carried off Mom's pencils and her fingernail polish and even her shoes! She was always looking for stuff that you had hidden."

"I know," Alexander said. "I sure had a lot to learn. So my Mommy said I needed to go to school."

"You went to school with children?" I asked.

"No, I went to school with other puppies. The school was called 'Dog Obedience.' My teacher, Ms. Arrington, was so nice."

I remembered that I went to school when I was a puppy, too. And I told Alexander that it surely helped me learn how to act.

"Yes, I learned lots," said Alexander. "I learned to sit, lay down, stay, and come when my name was called. I also learned not to hide Mommy's things, and to play with my own toys."

"School is **very** important," I said. "Not only for dogs, but for children too. That's where you learn important things that will help you take care of yourself when you grow up."

Alexander said. "I know so much now. And because I learned my lessons well, I was able to graduate. I wore a graduation cap and received a diploma."

"What's a diploma?" asked Katy.

Alexander said. "It's a certificate that says you've completed your lessons. It is an honor to graduate. Children get diplomas in grade 12 when they graduate from high school."

I asked Alexander to tell me how he felt when he graduated from school.

He said, "I was so happy and proud of myself."

I told him, "Alexander, I noticed that you told us about your school honor without bragging. It's important not to act better than anyone else. No one likes to hear others brag about themselves. You told us how happy you were with yourself without acting stuck up.

"Let's find Mom and see if she has any ideas on how to work on keeping ourselves happy."

Alexander found Mom and said, "Mommy, we like to feel happy. Like I felt when I graduated from school. Are there things that dogs, cats, and children can do to try to stay happy as long as possible?"

Mom answered, "There sure are. But first, remember that life has its ups and its downs. One day you may feel sad about something. Another day you may be confused about a decision. And the next day you may feel great—everything just seems to go perfect. Don't get **too** sad or **too** mad—because things will get better. Sometimes it just takes time for problems to be solved."

"That's good advice," I said. "It's really important to keep trying to have a better day. If you go about **a lot** with a mad face or a sad face, people won't want to be around you. Work on having a good attitude inside, and soon you'll be feeling OK."

Our days have Ups and Downs

Sunday	Monday	Tuesday	Wednesday	Thursday	Friday	Saturday
1 Happy Day!	2	3 ☺	4 Nervous about spelling words.	5	6	7 Nothing to do. I'm bored.
8	9 sad day	10 I'm excited!	11	12	13 I hurt my knee when I fell.	14
15 OK Day	16	17	18	19 I'm confused about a decision	20	21 ☺
22	23 Awesome!	24	25 Mad at my friend.	26	27 Great day.	28
29 ☹	30					

Mom said there are more things that you can do to try to keep feeling good. Here is her list:

☆ Always tell the truth. Then you won't ever feel bad for lying.

☆ Remember that no one else can make you mad or sad or confused or scared. **You** let yourself feel those ways. And if you don't want to feel those bad feeling for long, then get to work! Do whatever you can to change your feelings into better ones. It could be to give yourself a pep talk. Think of how hard you worked on your spelling words—even if your grade was low. It could be to get your mind off someone who called you a name. Forget him or her! There are lots of other people to play with. If you're sad, get involved in an activity you like. If you're scared to talk in front of the class, practice at home in front of the mirror to get over your fear. Or if you've made a mistake, figure out **how** not to make that same mistake again!

☆ Another way to keep feeling good is to give nice compliments to people you know. Instead of laughing at a classmate who gave a wrong answer in class, give that person a compliment at recess about how much fun he or she is. People don't like people who put others down. Give **"put-ups,"** not "put-downs." This will help you make, and keep, more friends.

☆ Learn to be good at talking to others. Don't just talk about yourself all the time. Be interested in people! Look at them when they talk to you. Listen closely. Don't interrupt. Ask when their birthday is, what sport they play or like best, or any of a million other questions you could ask them.

☆ And, as we said earlier in the book, keep a journal of positive thoughts about yourself. If each day you write down something that you feel good about, you'll find that you feel happier. You'll be glad that you are a nice, kind person.

☆ Remember, not **everyone** is going to like you. Some people will be your very best friends. Some people will be friends. And then there will always be someone who, for no reason at all, won't like you. Try not to let it bother you. Don't ever let anyone cause you to think less of yourself! Like yourself! Be yourself!

Chapter 7
Thinking about Our Feelings

How do you think I feel?

Let's think about the five feelings that my brothers, sisters, and I have talked about in this book. Those feelings are:

1. Confused
2. Sad
3. Mad
4. Scared
5. Happy

We're now going to play a game that will help us discuss our feelings. For each of the five feelings, I want you to name two words that mean about the same thing. For example, two other words that mean **happy** are **good** and **excited.**

Read on to begin the game.

When I feel **confused**, it's the same as feeling _____
or _____ .

Now think of a time when you've felt that way. Write about
it, or draw a picture about it. How did you get rid of the confused
feeling?

_____

_____

_____

_____

_____

When I feel **sad**, it means I feel _____ or

_____ .

Think of a time when you were sad. Write about it, or draw a picture of that time. What did you do to become less sad?

_____

_____

_____

_____

_____

Other words for **mad** are feeling _____ or

_____ .

When have you felt mad? Did you try to make the mad feeling go away, or did you let it control you? What are your favorite ways to calm yourself down when you feel mad?

_____

_____

_____

_____

_____

_____

Think of when you've been **scared**. Other words to describe feeling scared would be feeling _____ or _____ .

When have you felt scared? Write down how you became less scared, or explain by drawing a picture. Is it OK to feel scared?

_____

_____

_____

_____

_____

_____

When you're **happy**, you could say you feel _____ or
_____.

Write down, or draw, three times that you have felt happy.

_____

_____

_____

_____

_____

_____

Chapter 8
Practice Helps Us Learn

Mom and I are practicing with
students at a school.

You've learned a lot about feelings! You've learned how to control your feelings and try to be a happier person.

In Katy's story, we learned to get rid of confused feelings.

Cedric taught us how to deal with feeling sad.

Mandy taught us how to control our temper and not get so mad.

I taught us about what to do when we're scared.

And little Alexander taught us how to work hard at being happy.

Now let's read five stories about children who had problems with these feelings. This will give us a chance to practice what we've learned. We'll become problem-solvers!

Suzi's Story

"Is It My Fault?"

Suzi was playing in her room when suddenly she heard loud voices coming from the kitchen. She left her toys and walked into the hallway. Then Suzi stood very still. She could tell that her mommy and daddy were having a big argument.

She wondered if the argument was her fault. Could she have done something wrong that had caused her parents to get mad at each other and yell?

Suzi was confused and didn't know what to do.

Before you read the next page, answer what you think Suzi should do to get rid of her confused feelings.

"Understanding Adults Is Difficult"

Suzi remembered that asking questions and talking were some ways to get rid of confused feelings. So later that evening, she talked to each of her parents.

She asked her mother, "Were you and daddy arguing about me? I don't like it when you yell."

Her mother looked surprised and answered, "No, honey, we were talking about money. It was grown-up stuff that we were discussing. Sometimes adults get loud when they're talking about something that upsets them. It doesn't mean that we hate each other. We're just disagreeing. And you're right. We can disagree in a normal tone of voice."

When Suzi talked to her daddy about this, he said, "Suzi, you don't cause your mother and me to argue. We both love you so much."

Suzi was glad she had this talk with her parents. It can be tough trying to understand parents sometimes!

Ask questions and talk things out to help make confused feelings go away.

Victor's Story

"The Misunderstanding"

It was the first day of school. Victor was excited about meeting his new teacher and making new friends. Victor was paying attention in class and the day was going great.

Recess came and he invited some other boys to a game of kickball. They were having fun. Victor wondered how much longer recess would last, so he yelled to his teacher, "Ms. Bones, how much longer do we have to play?"

Everyone started laughing and pointing at him. "What's wrong?" Victor asked.

Rafael said, "The teacher's name is Jones, not Bones! You're stupid!" The students laughed loud—and long. Victor was sad. His feelings were hurt.

Victor's first day of school was turning into a disaster. Before you read the next page, answer what you would do if you were Victor.

" Ha! Ha! The Joke's on You!"

Victor quickly decided that he wasn't going to let anyone ruin his first day of school. He knew he wasn't stupid. He had simply made a mistake! No big deal! So he started laughing, too. Then his friends weren't laughing **at** him—but **with** him.

He said to the teacher, "I'm sorry that I heard your name wrong when I met you. Let me try again. How much longer until recess is over, Ms. **Jones**?"

She laughed and said, "Victor, you've got such a good sense of humor. It's going to be fun having you in my class."

Victor took control of how he wanted to feel. Every day Victor had been writing down a positive thought in his journal. He thought it made him stronger and able to handle any teasing that came his way.

Feel the way you want to feel. People who feel small put down others to feel big. Everyone makes mistakes—except people who are afraid to try!

Morgan's Story

"The Terrible, Yucky, Bad Day"

Even breakfast started off badly. Morgan's brother kept sticking his tongue out at her. That made her angry, so she hit him. Then her mother fussed at her for hitting. When Morgan tried to explain, her mother said, "Go straight to you room when you get home from school. You know hitting is not allowed—no excuses. Hurry! There's your bus."

It started to rain just as Morgan got off the school bus. She slipped on the wet sidewalk, and her spelling papers fell out of her book and blew away. Morgan knew the teacher would be disappointed that she didn't have her homework. Could this day get any worse? Yes.

At recess, Morgan got into an argument with her best friend, Natasha, about who was smarter. Morgan was upset that Natasha had called her an unkind name. Now they were not talking to each other.

Morgan was mad at a lot of people. She was very grumpy because of this terrible day. Before you read the next page, answer how you would try to make the rest of this day—and tomorrow—better.

"Happy Days Are Here Again"

When Morgan got home from school, she was told to go to her room, and she did. Instead of just sitting alone and sulking, she decided to hold her teddy bear and think about how she could make herself feel better. She came up with some great ideas.

First, she drew a pretty picture for her mother and wrote on it: "I'm sorry that I hit my brother. Next time I'll ask you for help before I lose my temper."

Then she apologized to her brother for hitting him. She also asked him to leave her alone in the morning because she's sleepy and doesn't like to be teased. He said OK, although Morgan knew he might forget some days and still tease her. She knew she was big enough to ignore his silly teasing.

Then Morgan called her best friend and said, "Natasha, I want us to have fun at school tomorrow. Both of us are smart. You're really good at spelling and dancing. I'm really good at math and running fast. Let's forget our silly argument."

Natasha said, "OK," but still sounded upset. Morgan knew that most arguments between good friends don't last more than one day. She was sure that they would play at recess tomorrow and have a good time.

The last thing Morgan did was read a funny story before bedtime. She laughed a lot before she fell asleep.

Don't hold your mad feelings inside. Do figure out OK ways to get out your mad feelings and make your day better—like Morgan did.

Carson's Story

"The Move"

When Carson's mom told him that she had a new job and would make more money, he was excited. He wasn't excited for long, though, because he learned that this would mean they would move far away from the home where they had always lived. He would have to leave his school, his friends, and his neighborhood.

Carson began having bad dreams because he was so scared about moving.

Before you read the next page, decide what you think Carson should do to get rid of his scared feelings.

"Sweet Dreams Can Come True"

Carson thought he probably should talk to his mom about this. He called for her late one night, and she opened his bedroom door.

"What is it, Carson?" she asked.

"I'm scared about our moving."

His mother answered, "I am, too, Carson. Let's talk about it. It's always scary when we do new things and we're not sure how they'll turn out. Why don't we go visit the new town where we're moving?"

"That's a great idea," said Carson. "Can we drive by my new school?"

"Sure," his mom answered. "And I'll try to find out your new teacher's name. You can write to her and your new classmates and tell them about yourself. Maybe some will write back to you, and then you'll have some friends before you even arrive! It's time to go to sleep now. We'll plan this tomorrow. Goodnight."

Carson fell asleep right away and had sweet dreams.

Talk about your feelings to an adult whom you trust. Doing this can help make bad feelings go away.

Tyler's Story

"The Championship Game"

Tyler was so excited! His softball team had won so many games that they were going to get to play for the city championship. If they won, they would be the best team in the whole city! Today was the big game. He and his teammates were ready.

His team played hard. They made no mistakes. Tyler even got a home run! But, in the end, the score was 6 for the other team and 5 for Tyler's team. They lost by only one point.

Tyler's coach was upset and fussing at the boys for not playing hard enough. But Tyler knew they **had** played their best. That day the other team just played a little better. Tyler was happy with himself and proud of his team.

Tyler felt good. Before you read the next page, decide if Tyler should let his coach's attitude change how he feels.

"The Choice"

Tyler likes to feel good. He knew that he and his teammates had honestly played their very best. But that day the other team played better. So there was no reason to feel bad.

Tyler **chose** to feel good. He walked over to the bleachers where the parents were sitting. His father said, "Son, that was a great home run. I'm proud of you."

Tyler smiled. It was a good day.

Decide to feel good as often as possible. Don't let others change your up feelings into down ones! Be in control of your own emotions!

Chapter 9
It's Been Fun!

Having fun with friends!

It's been fun talking with you again. I hope that you learned more about life. As Mom says, it has its ups and its downs.

You're not going to be happy all of the time. Not everyone's going to like you all of the time. But that's how life is—for **all** of us. Try to change the bad, grumpy days into better ones. Enjoy the good days!

Before I say good-bye, there are a few last things that I want to say to you . . .

1. Be kind to others. Be friendly. Say hi to all the other kids. You can have more than one friend, so don't get jealous when your friend also has more than one friend.

   P.S. Be kind to animals, too!

Mom and I are making friends with a mama duck and her 19 babies!

2. If you have brothers and sisters, try to really like them. Don't worry about your parents liking one of you the best. They love you **all**! Each of you is different and special in your own way.

Alexander can be a pest, but I really love him.

3. When you're having a terrible, yucky, bad, stinking-rotten day, ask for a hug from an adult whom you trust. It will remind you that you're a special person and that someone cares about you.

Mom gives me a big hug.

4. Share your feelings with your parent or grandparents or teachers or other adults whom you trust. Get those down feelings out in the open so that they can go away.

Sharing my feelings with Mom.

Our days are like the weather. Some days are sunny and bright. Some days are cloudy and cold. Others are stormy. And some days even have a rainbow!

Mom and I wish you lots of beautiful, sunny days with **many** rainbows!

Love,

Nicholas

Ending Note to Parents and Teachers

Use *Life's Not Always Fair* with your child or student to begin lots of discussion about, and practice in, how to manage emotions. Some suggested follow-up ideas:

1. When watching television with your child, note when the characters fail to control their emotions. Ask the child if there were other ways that the characters could have solved their problems.
2. Avoid negating your child's feelings with remarks such as, "You shouldn't feel that way." The feeling is the real way your child feels. Don't deny the feelings or your child will soon quit expressing them. Do help your child learn to change down feelings into better ones.
3. In the process of developing the skills discussed in this book, the child may need your guidance. If the child is having difficulty overcoming a fear or calming down, you may have to suggest that the child go think over his or her options. After 15 minutes or so, see if the child has come up with some ideas. Also, some children are too timid at first to talk about their feelings. If this is a problem, ask the child to express his or her ideas by writing about them or by drawing them.
4. Use words to describe your feelings when talking to your child. Avoid saying that nothing is wrong when the child can clearly see that you're upset. You don't have to give all the details, but you can say things such as, "I'm nervous because I have to go for a job interview tomorrow," or "Your dad and I are upset with each other over a bill." Assure your child that you are trying to change your bad mood into a better one.
5. Give praise anytime you see the child maintain control over negative emotions and use the skills learned in this book. Make the praise **100% positive** by stating what the child did

well, such as, "I noticed you thought before you spoke. You did a good job controlling your anger." (**Not** "You didn't lose your temper like last time.")

6. Reward your children or students with tokens whenever you hear them give a sincere "put-up" (compliment) to others. Let them redeem a certain number of the tokens for small prizes.

7. Supply them with more hypothetical situations, similar to those in Chapter 8, to give them the opportunity to practice their skills. Make the situations appropriate to their frame of reference. For example, many children are terrified of drive-by shootings or being offered drugs on the way to school. That's a reality in their neighborhoods, so provide them with situations which reflect that reality. Remember: encourage them to think on their own. Make them come up with ways to handle the situation; do not tell them how you would deal with it, except as a last resort.

8. Have your child or student write to Nicholas and tell him what he or she learned from this book. His address is on page 110, and Nicholas always answers his mail.

9. Be a role model by dealing with your fears, anger, confusion, and sadness in constructive ways. If the child or student sees you frequently "blow your top" when you lose your temper, then he or she is going to learn that this is the way to deal with frustration. If your child sees you throw things when you are confused, do not be surprised when you see him or her exhibit the same behavior. When you receive a compliment from others, don't negate it with replies such as "Anyone could do it" or "It's no big deal." Let the child see you accept good feelings with a "Thank you." Children do as we do, rather than do what we tell them to do!

Public Service Footnote

Nicholas' diagnosis of nasal cancer was discussed in Chapter 5, and as the details of his illness may prove helpful to you, I feel it is important to share them. Based on information gleaned from his lab biopsy, and considering the timing of the onset of his symptoms, it is believed that the nasal cancer can be traced to the application in our neighborhood's greenbelt areas of an herbicide called 2,4-D. An article in the *Journal of the National Cancer Institute*, "Herbicides and Cancer," December 16, 1992, concludes that "there is reasonable evidence to suggest that herbicide exposure results in an increased risk of developing non-Hodgkin's lymphoma" and "some data suggest a link between herbicide exposure and cancers of the colon, lung, nose, prostate and ovary as well as leukemia and multiple myeloma." The article calls for more studies and public education. As a result, the Environmental Protection Agency, along with the National Cancer Institute, have instituted a 10-year, $15 million study of this chemical. The *Registry of Toxic Effects of Chemical Substances* already lists 2,4-D as a carcinogen.

2,4-D is one of the most common lawn-care pesticides currently in use. It is found in 1,500 products on the market! So that what has happened to Nicholas does not happen to you, your child, or your pet, be careful about the use of chemicals in your yard. Contrary to popular thinking, the danger of the chemical is **not** over when it dries. Consider going organic in your lawn care! I did in 1987 and found it easier and less expensive! Please contact me if you have trouble finding information on how to become an organic gardener. I'll be more than happy to help you.

Thank you.

Sharon Scott

Ordering Other Books by Sharon Scott

Contact:

Human Resource Development Press
22 Amherst Rd.
Amherst, MA 01002 U.S.A.
1-800-822-2801 (U.S. and Canada)
413-253-3488 (other countries)
(413) 253-3490 (fax)
http://www.hrdpress.com

for information on ordering:

- **Peer Pressure Reversal: An Adult Guide to Developing a Responsible Child** (2nd edition)
- **Too Smart for Trouble** with Nicholas, the Cocker Spaniel (grades K-4)
- **Not Better . . . Not Worse . . . Just Different** with Nicholas, the Cocker Spaniel (grades K-5)
- **Too Cool for Drugs**, with Wayne Hindmarsh, Ph.D., and Nicholas, the Cocker Spaniel (grades 1-5)
- **How to Say No and Keep Your Friends** (grades 5-12)
- **Positive Peer Groups** (for adults)
- **When to Say Yes! And Make More Friends** (grades 5-12)

Quantity discounts are available. Call for details.

Consider bringing Sharon Scott to your community to speak to students, parents, or educators on **Life's Not Always Fair** or one of her 29 skills-based topics, including:

- **Peer Pressure Reversal—Teaching Children and Teens to Think on Their Own**
- **Too Cool for Drugs**
- **How to Say No and Keep Your Friends**
- **Positive Peer Groups: Kids Helping Kids**

Write for more information:

Sharon Scott (and Nicholas)
Windy Star Ranch
P. O. Box 6
Weston, TX   75097-0006

Ordering the Nicholas Hand Puppet and Teaching Transparencies

Use this darling, 14-inch hand puppet as a teaching resource to enhance learning. To order, send a purchase order or a check for $29.95 to Ms. Scott at the above address.

Teaching transparencies are also available for this book (and the other three by Nicholas). $49.95 per set. Specify which book title you want and send purchase order or check to Ms. Scott at the address above.